A SIMPLE
INTRODUCTION TO
CHEMISTRY

BY MAX
PARSONAGE

Published by Max Parsonage
12 Long Lane, Littlemore, Oxford, England
UK OX4 3TW
© Max Parsonage 2013(eBook)
© Max Parsonage 2018 (this book)

ISBN 978-0-9555451-4-6

Table of Contents

A simple introduction to chemistry

This book explains the core ideas in chemistry in plain English. All chemistry depends on these core ideas. In chemistry, the ideas build up layer upon layer, so this book is best read in the order that it is written. Many practice questions are included, to help you check that you comprehend the ideas.

How to study chemistry and succeed

To succeed you must **understand** the basic ideas and not just memorise the facts. By understanding these principles, and the patterns within chemistry, you will be able to predict many chemical formulas and reactions.

The ideas in chemistry build up layer upon layer, so study them in the order they are written. Use the questions to check that you really do understand the concepts.

Good luck with your studies!

Max Parsonage, 2013.

About chemistry

Chemistry is the study of matter, the different types of materials that make up the world around us, and how to change one type of matter into another.

You may be studying chemistry at school, or about to study a subject related to chemistry, or perhaps you wish to understand chemistry having missed chemistry earlier in your life. Chemistry will enable to you comprehend many situations around you in everyday life, in the home and at work, also environmental issues, technology, agriculture, geology, engineering, biology, and medicine. Chemicals, good and bad, make up our food, materials, fabrics, cosmetics, batteries, water, phones, and the air we breath. Life is richer when you can visualize the molecular world.

About the printed version
Originally, I planned only to make the eBook version. The many wonderful compliments that people posted online gladdened this writer's heart. There were requests for a paper version and I came to realise that, in reality, many thirteen year olds prefer paper books to eBooks.

I do hope that this small book helps many people to comprehend chemistry.
Max Parsonage, 2018, Oxford, England, UK

Start here

To start with, all you need to know is that an electrical charge may be positive (+) or negative (-). Also that, positive and negative charges attract each other, and the same charges repel. For example two particles with negative charges will repel each other.

What are atoms?

Everything around you is made of small particles called **atoms**. These atoms are so small that around 10 000 000 000 could fit along a one metre (one yard) desk edge. There are many different types of atoms and they join in different ways to make the different substances.

Atoms cannot be split except inside a sun, or in a nuclear bomb or reactor. They have an internal structure, and it is this structure that changes during chemical reactions.

What is atomic structure?

Atoms have structure. The central **nucleus** contains positively charged **protons** (+) and neutral **neutrons** (0) and is surrounded by layers, called **shells**, of negatively charged **electrons** (–). The electron number is equal to the proton number (atomic number) in a **neutral** (uncharged) atom. In other words one plus charge neutralizes one negative charge. **Atoms are neutral** because the number of positive protons equals the number of negative electrons. The protons attract the electrons because they have opposite charges.

Here is a simple atom with one proton in the nucleus and one electron in an electron shell:

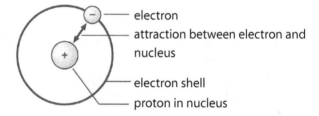

A lithium atom has three protons (+), three electrons (-) and, not shown here, four neutrons (0):

Electrons are negative. They have a very small mass. The electrons are found in layers, called shells, around the nucleus. They are attracted to the positive protons in the nucleus.

Protons are positive. They have mass and are found in the nucleus of an atom. The positive protons attract the negative electrons.

Neutrons are neutral, and they have no charge. They have roughly the same mass as the protons, and they are found in the nucleus. The neutrons help to bind the protons together in the nucleus.

Remember: **P**rotons are **P**ositive.
Neutrons are **Neutr**al. Electrons are negative.

> **Neutrons** do not affect the chemistry, only the mass of the atoms, so, in this book, they are not shown in the diagrams.

Practice questions 1: Atomic structure
1. For each particle inside the atom, state the **mass** and then the **charge**:
2. Why does the nucleus attract electrons?
3. Why are atoms neutral?
4. What is the name given to the layers of electrons around an atom?
5. What is the name given to the middle of an atom?
6. Which are the particles inside the atom that have mass one?

Answers to practice questions 1

1. proton mass 1 charge +1, neutron mass 1 no charge, electron negligible mass – 1 charge
2. because the positive protons in the nucleus attract the negative electrons
3. because the number of electrons equal the number of protons
4. shells
5. nucleus
6. protons and neutrons

What are elements?

The simplest type of chemical is called an **element**. Each element contains one type of atom. For example, the element copper only contains copper atoms.

Here, to illustrate the idea of elements, are graphical representations of some elements using the symbols that were used two hundred years ago:

An element only contains only one type of atom

hydrogen
atoms

carbon
atoms

oxygen
atoms

magnesium
atoms

Actually atoms of the same element have the same number of protons in every nucleus. For example, all carbon atoms contain six protons; all hydrogen atoms contain one proton; all copper atoms contain 29 protons. All this will be discussed in more detail later.

Elements are the simplest chemicals. An element cannot be made any simpler because it only contains one type of atom.

There are over one hundred different types of atoms, **and so elements. Most of them are metals. The rest are** called non-metals.

Different elements combine to form compounds.

Practice questions 2: Elements
1. What are elements?
2. All atoms of the same element have the same number of, what?
3. Roughly how many elements are there?
4. Most elements are, what?
5. Atoms of different elements have different numbers of, what?

Answers to practice questions 2
1. pure substances that contain one sort of atom
2. protons in the nucleus.
3. over one hundred
4. metals
5. protons in the nucleus.

What are compounds and mixtures?

A **compound** is formed when two, or more, elements are chemically joined. **Example:** water is a compound made of the elements hydrogen and oxygen. The atoms of these two elements are chemically joined together. To illustrate the idea of compounds, here are representations of some compounds using the old symbols:

Compounds contain more than one type of atom

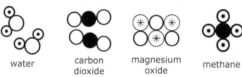

| water | carbon dioxide | magnesium oxide | methane |

The atoms in compounds, and in most elements, are chemically joined together. A join between atoms is called a **chemical bond**.

Physically mixing elements only produces a **mixture**, in that the different sorts of particles in mixtures just lay next to each other. **Example:** the air is made of the elements nitrogen, oxygen and argon (with other chemicals). These elements are physically mixed together. They are not chemically joined together. Again, here are some examples:

Mixtures contain more than one type of chemical

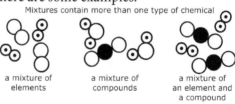

a mixture of elements | a mixture of compounds | a mixture of an element and a compound

Practice questions 3: Elements, compounds and mixtures

1. Atoms of different elements have different numbers of, what?
2. What are elements?
3. What are compounds?
4. What is a mixture?
5. Which type of substance has only one type of atom?
6. Which type of substance is formed from different elements that are chemically combined?
7. Which type of substance contains different types of atoms that are chemically joined?

Answers to practice questions 3

1. protons in the nucleus
2. pure substances that contain one sort of atom
3. atoms of two, or more, elements are not just mixed together but chemically combined.
4. A mixture is when two or more chemicals (elements or compounds) are physically mixed.
5. elements
6. compounds
7. compounds

What is the Periodic Table?

There are over one hundred elements, and they are usually presented as the 'periodic table', which reflects the detailed structure of the different atoms. The periodic table is organized in the order of the number of protons in the nucleus, which is called 'the atomic number'. This means that hydrogen is the first element with one proton in each nucleus, helium two, lithium three and so on. The periodic table will be more fully explained later.

On the next page is a periodic table showing the first 20 elements.

The full periodic table is at the back of this book, or you could find one online.

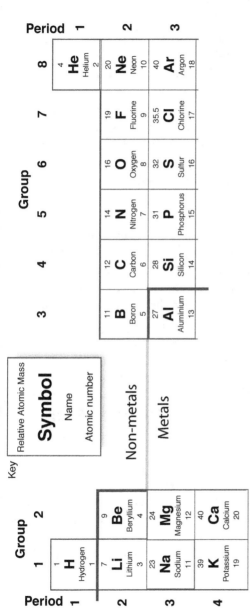

Here is a part of the Periodic Table showing the first twenty elements. Really, there are over 100.

A full periodic table is printed at the back of this book.

Note that usually at school level only eight groups (columns) are labeled 1 - 8, while at degree level the eighteen groups (columns) are labelled 1 - 18.

Usually each element is given a box in the periodic table. The element symbol is shown with two numbers. One number is the **atomic number** (the number of protons) and the other is the Relative Atomic Mass, which is explained below.

The mass of each atom is equal to the number of protons + neutrons. This is called the **mass number**. Actually the mass number of an element's atoms varies, because the number of neutrons varies. These atoms of an element that have a different number of neutrons, but the same number of protons, are called **isotopes**.

The average mass of the atoms of an element is called the **Relative Atomic Mass** (RAM). One unit of RAM, the atomic unit (a.u.), is equal to one twelfth the mass of a carbon-12 atom. (Carbon-12 means a carbon atom with mass number 12.)

Remember:
The larger number is always
        the Relative Atomic **Mass**,
so remember that RAM is the more **massive**.

The elements that make up the periodic table are either metals or non-metals.

What are metals and non-metals?

Most of the elements are metals. Look at the periodic table **at the back of the book**. The twenty-two **non-metals** are the elements to the right and above of the thick black line. The element hydrogen, over on the left, is also a non-metal. The rest are **metals**.

Practice questions 4: The Periodic Table, metals and non-metals

1. How is the periodic table organized?
2. How many of the elements are metals?
3. In the periodic table, the metals are mainly found, where?
4. The modern periodic table is arranged in order of what?
5. What is the mass number equal to?
6. What is meant by the 'Atomic Number'?
7. What is the number of protons in an atom called?
8. What is the number of protons plus neutrons called?
9. What is meant by the Relative Atomic Mass?
10. Atoms of the same element that have different number of neutrons are called, what?
11. State the correct number of particles in a sodium atom and give the electron structure. (Note sodium is Atomic Number 11 and Mass Number 23)
12. What are isotopes?
13. Where are the non-metals found in the periodic table?

Answers to practice questions 4

1. generally in order of the proton number, which is called the atomic number
2. three-quarters
3. in the central block and in the first two columns
4. the atomic number
5. the number of protons plus neutrons
6. the number of protons
7. the atomic number
8. the mass number
9. the average mass of the atoms of an element
10. isotopes
11. 11 protons 12 neutrons 11 electrons: electron structure 2,8,1.
12. atoms with the same number of protons but different number of neutrons
13. on the right (and include hydrogen which is on the left) above the dark line

What is bonding in chemistry?

There are three ways that the particles in elements and compounds bond together. The three types of bonding are called, **metallic**, **ionic** and **covalent** bonding.

There are three types of particles: **atoms**, **ions**, and **molecules**.

Ions are charged particles so may be charged positive(+) or negative(-). Ions form when a neutral atom gains or loses electrons.

Molecules are groups of atoms joined together by covalent bonds (see page 17).

What is metallic bonding?
Metallic bonding only occurs in metals. Here, the negative electrons in the outer shells are free to move, leaving the central atoms positively charged. This diagram represents metallic bonding:

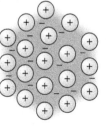

When just metal atoms join together then metallic bonds form.

Remember:

METAL + METAL = METALLIC

Positive ions are called **cations**. Metallic bonding may be described as 'cations in a sea of mobile negative electrons'. In metals, electricity is the flow of these mobile electrons.

You could remember that, 'CATions are PUSSYtive':

Metals are either pure, so only contain one type of atom, or are made of a mixture of metal atoms which are called **alloys**.

Example: pure gold only contains gold atoms.

Example: the alloy bronze is a mixture made of copper and tin atoms.

What is ionic bonding?

When one atom loses an electron to another atom then ions are formed, so **ionic bonding** occurs. **Ions** are charged particles in that they have either a positive (+) charge or a negative(-) charge.

As electrons are negative, when a neutral atom gains a negative electron then a negative ion is formed, which is called an **anion**. In contrast, when a neutral atom loses a negative electron then a positive ion is formed, which is called a **cation**. These positive and negative ions are attracted together because oppositely charged ions attract (and ions with the same charge repel). This strong force of attraction is called **electrostatic force**. All this describes ionic bonding.

In other words, **ionic bonding** is when there is a complete **transfer** of electrons from one atom to another atom, to form oppositely charged ions, which are held together by a strong electrostatic force. This transfer of electrons occurs in some chemical reactions.

Usually it is metallic atoms that lose electrons to become positively charged ions, and it is non-metal atoms that gain electrons to become negatively charged ions.

Remember:
METAL + NON-METAL = IONIC

Example: sodium atoms react with chlorine. Sodium is a metal (with the symbol Na). Chlorine (Cl) is a non-metal. In the reaction each sodium atoms loses an electron to form a positive sodium ion with a one plus charge (Na^+), and each chlorine atom gains one electron to make a negative ion with a one minus charge (Cl^-). The compound formed is called sodium chloride. Note that when a compound forms then the ending on the non-metal changes. The ending 'ide' indicates that the non-metal is in the compound with the first element named.

This reaction may be written as a word equation:
sodium + chlorine $\rightarrow$ sodium chloride
or written as a symbol equation:
$Na + Cl \rightarrow Na^+ + Cl^-$

What is covalent bonding?

Another way that atoms join is by sharing electrons. Usually each atom donates one electron. A **covalent bond** is the sharing of an electron pair by two atoms. Both nuclei are attracted to the shared electrons in a covalent bond because the positive nuclei are attracted to the negative electrons:

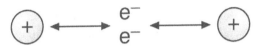

nuclei attracted to shared atoms

The diagram above represents nuclei attracted to shared electrons.

Generally when a covalent bond forms both the atoms are non-metal atoms. Both atoms could be from the same element, or one atom could be from one non-metal element and the other atom from another non-metal element.

Remember:

NON-METAL + NON-METAL = COVALENT

Example: In a sample of the element hydrogen, two hydrogen atoms are joined together to form a covalent bond. Each hydrogen atom has one electron. Each atom donates their one electron to the other atom to form a covalent bond. Here then, the two hydrogen atoms share an electron pair.

Example: Some hydrogen and chlorine react together to form a sample of the compound hydrogen chloride. Each hydrogen atom shares their one electron with a chlorine atom to form a covalent bond. Similarly, each chlorine atom shares one of their electrons with a hydrogen atom.

This may be written as a word equation:

hydrogen atom + chlorine atom → hydrogen chloride molecule

or as a symbol equation:

$$H + Cl \rightarrow HCl$$

Practice questions 5: Bonding

1. When metal atoms react with non-metals atoms, what type of bonding occurs?

2. Why do covalently bonded atoms stay together?

3. What type of bonding may be described as 'positive ions in a sea of mobile electrons'?

4. When atoms form chemical bonds by gaining and losing electrons they form, what?

5. What type of bonding may be described as 'the complete transfer of electrons to form oppositely charged ions held together by strong electrostatic forces'?

6. Why do the ions stay together in an ionic compound?

7. Atoms that lose electrons become, what?

8 Metals and non-metals react to form, what?

9. Atoms that gain electrons form, what?

10. How do atoms form chemical bonds?

11. Why do metal atoms stick together?

12. What type of bonding occurs when 'two atoms share an electron pair '?

13. When non-metal atoms react with non-metal atoms, what type of bonding occurs?

14. When metal atoms react with metal atoms, what type of bonding occurs?

15. Which particles are ionic compounds made of?

16. Two different metal atoms make, what?

Answers to practice questions 5

1. ionic bonding
2. Both nuclei are attracted to the shared electrons.
3. metallic bonding
4. electrically charged atoms called ions
5. ionic bonding
6. Oppositely charged ions are attracted together by strong electrostatic forces.
7. positively charged
8 ionic compounds
9. negative ions
10. only by gaining or losing electrons, or by sharing electrons
11 In metals the outer electrons are mobile. This leaves positive ions that are attracted to the mobile electrons.
12. covalent bonding
13. covalent bonding
14. metallic bonding
15. ions
16. mix together to form an alloy

Note: The shells are actually Energy Levels.
The term "shells" is used here as it is easier for new students of chemistry to comprehend.

The electronic structure of atoms

The arrangement of the electrons inside each atom, the electronic structure, more fully explains bonding. Remember that in an atom the number of positive protons equals the number of negative electrons, so atoms are always **neutral**.

Hydrogen is the simplest atom. It has one proton in the nucleus and so one electron around the outside. One way of representing a hydrogen atom is to draw a 'one plus' sign to represent the one proton, and a circle to represent the first shell, with one electron in the first shell.

This represents a hydrogen atom:

Helium's atoms contain two protons, so it is the second element in the periodic table. Two protons mean that helium atoms have two electrons around the outside:

These diagrams may be called, Bohr, or **Lewis diagrams,** or even 'D**ot & Cross Diagram**s', because some people handdraw dots and crosses to represent the negative electrons.

Here is an example of a hand drawn dot and cross diagram for lithium fluoride:

Lithium has three protons, and so has three electrons around the outside. This time two electrons fit in the first shell and one electron fits in the next shell, because the first shell can only hold up to two electrons. The electronic structure may be written as 2,1, or drawn as:

Similarly, beryllium has four protons, boron five, carbon six. Written as Be 2,2; B 2,3; C 2,4; and drawn as:

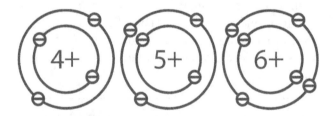

Note that the number of protons is called the atomic number, and the elements are arranged in the periodic table in the order of the atomic number (proton number).

The next elements are nitrogen with seven protons, oxygen with eight, fluorine with nine and neon with ten. Written as N 2,5; O 2,6; F 2,7; Ne 2,8; and drawn as:

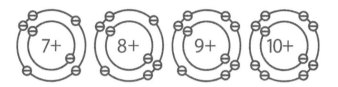

The next element is sodium with eleven protons. As only up to eight electrons may fit into the second shell, in sodium atoms a new shell is started by adding one electron to the third shell. Written as 2,8,1; drawn as:

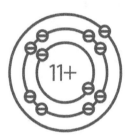

A chlorine atom has an atomic number of 17, so has seventeen protons, is written as Cl 2, 8, 7; and drawn as:

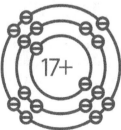

Though drawing these diagrams is a useful way to understand electronic structure, there is another way to show electronic structure, and that is by listing the number of electrons in each shell. In this way sodium's electronic structure would be [2, 8,1] and chlorine's would be [2, 8, 7].

Here is a table showing the electronic structure for the early elements:

atomic number (proton number)	element name	symbol	electronic structure
1	Hydrogen	H	[1]
2	Helium	He	[2]
3	Lithium	Li	[2, 1]
4	Beryllium	Be	[2, 2]
5	Boron	B	[2, 3]
6	Carbon	C	[2, 4]
7	Nitrogen	N	[2, 5]
8	Oxygen	O	[2, 6]
9	Fluorine	F	[2, 7]
10	Neon	Ne	[2, 8]
11	Sodium	Na	[2, 8, 1]

Note that each time a new shell is started then a new row on the periodic table is started. In other words, the row number on the periodic table indicates the number of electron shells. Also note that the number of electrons that each shell may hold is reflected in the number of elements in each row of the periodic table.

It is the number of electrons in the outer shell that determine the chemical character of the element. As atoms of elements in the same group (column) have the same number of electrons in the outer shell, so elements in the same group have similar chemical behaviour. Atoms of elements in the same period (row) have the same number of electron shells.

As an exercise, it would be useful for you to draw out the electronic structures of the first twenty elements.

Here are the electronic structures of the rest of the first twenty elements:

atomic number (proton number)	element name	symbol	electronic structure
12	Magnesium	Mg	[2, 8, 2]
13	Aluminium	Al	[2, 8, 3]
14	Silicon	Si	[2, 8, 4]
15	Phosphorous	P	[2, 8, 5]
16	Sulfur	S	[2, 8, 6]
17	Chlorine	Cl	[2, 8, 7]
18	Argon	Ar	[2, 8, 8]
19	Potassium	K	[2, 8, 8, 1]
20	Calcium	Ca	[2, 8, 8, 2]

Electronic structure and ions

Sodium chloride, the common salt that we eat, is made of sodium ions and chloride ions. Sodium chloride may be made by reacting sodium with chlorine.

Note that the ending of the non-metal word is changed when used in a compound. Generally the word 'chlorine' in a compound changes to 'chloride', and 'oxygen' changes to 'oxide'.

Remember:
Ions are charged particles
in that they have either an overall positive (+) charge or a negative (-) charge.

A sodium atom, which has eleven protons (11+), has an electronic structure of [2,8,1] while a chlorine atom has seventeen protons (17+) and has an electronic structure of [2,8,7].

The following diagram shows the electronic structure of a sodium atom and a chlorine atom. (A different symbol for the electrons on the chlorine atom has been chosen to make this discussion clearer):

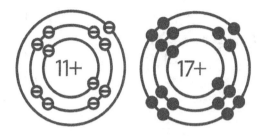

As sodium is a metal and chlorine a non-metal, then when they react each sodium atom loses an electron to a chlorine atom:

As the chlorine atom has gained a negative electron the chlorine atom now has a negative charge. It is important to understand and remember this. The sodium atom has lost a negative electron so now is a positive sodium ion:

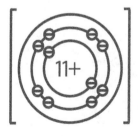 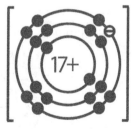

Remember that ions are charged particles. The charges on the ions are shown by adding square brackets, and the charge:

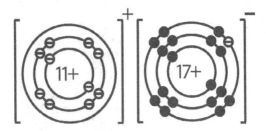

This is called sodium chloride. The word ending has changed to denote that the chlorine is in a compound.

Note that, as a general rule, after a reaction the atoms end up with **a full outer shell**, that is the highest number of electrons the shell can hold.

In the next example more than one electron is transferred. When the metal magnesium reacts with the non-metal fluorine then the magnesium atoms lose electrons to the fluorine.

Magnesium atoms have the electronic structure [2,8,2]:

So when magnesium atoms react they lose both the outer two electrons to the fluorine atoms to make magnesium ions with a structure of $[2,8,0]^{2+}$ (also written as $[2,8]^{2+}$):

Each fluorine atom, with an electronic structure of $[2,7]$ only has room for one electron in the outer shell:

Here then, one magnesium atom loses two electrons to two fluorine atoms, so that in magnesium fluoride there is one magnesium ion (symbol Mg^{2+}) for every two fluoride ions (symbol F^-)

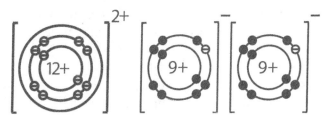

What would happen if sodium reacted with oxygen? The electronic structure of sodium is [2,8,1] and that of oxygen is [2,6]. Note that each oxygen atom has room for two electrons, so that two sodium atoms each lose one electron, and that the two electrons both go to one oxygen atom. So, two sodium ions (Na^+) join with one oxide ion (O^{2-}):

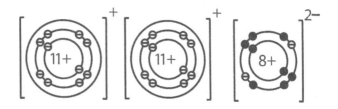

Remember:
When **metals and hydrogen** atoms react
then, generally, they **lose** electrons to form **positive ions**,

and, when **non-metal atoms** react,
generally, they **gain** electrons to form **negative ions** (unless the non-metals atoms are forming covalent bonds).

Also remember that, in general,
after a reaction, atoms end up with a full outer shell.

Practice questions 6: Electronic structure of atoms & ions

1. When metals react they generally make, what? Why?
2. When non-metal atoms react and form ions, what type of ions do they generally make? Why?
3. When hydrogen atoms react and form ions, what type of ions usually form?
4. Give the electronic structure for a sodium atom.
5. Give the electronic structure for a chlorine atom.
6. Give the electronic structure for a oxygen atom.
7. Give the electronic structure for a magnesium atom.
8 Give the electronic structure for a aluminium atom.
9. Give the electronic structure for a hydrogen atom.
10. Give the electronic structure for a lithium atom.
11 Give the electronic structure for a potassium atom.
12. Give the electronic structure for a nitrogen atom.
13. Give the electronic structure for the particles in sodium oxide;
14. Give the electronic structure for the particles in aluminium oxide;
15. Give the electronic structure for the particles in lithium fluoride;
16. Give the electronic structure for sodium chloride;
17. Give the electronic structure for magnesium oxide;
18 Give the electronic structure for calcium chloride;

Answers to practice questions 6

1. Metal atoms generally lose negative electrons and so form positive ions.

2. When forming ions, non-metal atoms gain negative electrons and so form negative ions.

3. When forming ions, hydrogen atoms generally lose one negative electron and so form positive ions.

4. $Na = [2,8,1]$

5. $Cl = [2,8,7]$

6. $O = [2,8,6]$

7. $Mg = [2,8,2]$

8 $Al = [2,8,3]$

9. $H = [1]$

10. $Li = [2,1]$

11. $K = [2,8,8,1]$

12. $N = [2,5]$

13. $2 \times (Na^+) = [2,8,8]^+$, $(O^{2-}) = [2,8]^{2-}$

14. $2 \times (Al^{3+}) = [2,8,8]^{3+}$, $3 \times (O^{2-}) = [2,8,8]^{2-}$

15. $(Li^+) = [2]^+$, $(F^-) = [2,8]^-$

16. $(Na^+) = [2,8]^+$, $(Cl^-) = [2,8,8]^-$

17. $(Mg^{2+}) = [2,8]^{2+}$, $(O^{2-}) = [2,8]^{2-}$

18. $(Ca^{2+}) = [2,8,8]^{2+}$, $2 \times (Cl^-) = [2,8,8]^-$

Note: Different symbols for electrons are used here to help show where the electrons are coming from. Actually, all electrons are identical.

Electronic structure and covalent molecules

When two non-metal atoms react together then they form a covalent bond. The simplest example of a covalent bond is in the element hydrogen. Here are two hydrogen atoms:

Each hydrogen atom has one electron in the outer shell. This is the innermost shell so it can only hold up to two electrons. When the two atoms join together both atoms share the electron pair:

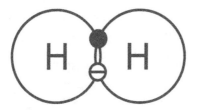

These two hydrogen atoms, joined together, form a small unit called a hydrogen molecule, symbol H_2. A **molecule** is a group of atoms joined together by covalent bonds.

Another example of a covalent bond is in the compound hydrogen chloride. Here is an atom of hydrogen and an atom of chlorine:

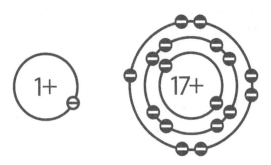

The chlorine atom has seven electrons in the outer shell, which may contain up to eight electrons. When the hydrogen and chlorine atoms join they each share one electron with the other atom. Note that in the process they fill their outer shells:

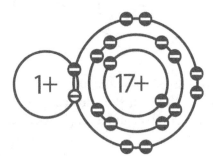

It is possible for molecules to contain more than two atoms. Water is a compound made from three atoms, one oxygen atom and two hydrogen atoms. Here are these atoms:

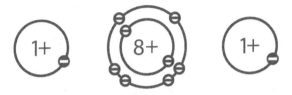

When they join then the central oxygen atom shares one electron with each hydrogen atom. Each hydrogen atom shares their one electron with the oxygen atom, and so in the process all the atoms gain a full outer shell:

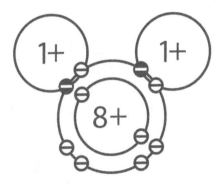

In this way the structure of a covalent molecule may be described using diagrams to show the electronic structure of the atoms.

Sometimes the positive charge in the nucleus is not shown. Instead, the symbol of the element is shown which indicates the proton number, as each element has only one atomic (proton) number. Oxygen atoms always have eight protons, and hydrogen atoms always have one proton. Here is an example of the symbols in use:

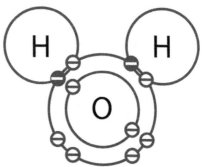

Sometimes, the inner electron shell is missed off, like this:

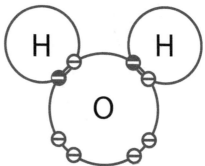

Practice questions 7: Electronic structure of atoms and covalent molecules

1. Give the electronic structure of a hydrogen atom.

2. Give the electronic structure of a carbon atom.

3. Give the electronic structure of a nitrogen atom.

4. Give the electronic structure of a oxygen atom.

5. Give the electronic structure of a fluorine atom.

6. Give the electronic structure of a chlorine atom.

7. Draw a dot and cross diagram to work out the formula of hydrogen chloride.

8. Draw a Lewis dot diagram (dot & cross diagram) for methane, CH_4. (Just draw the outer shells)

9. Draw a Lewis dot diagram for ammonia, NH_3. (Just draw the outer shells)

10. Draw a Lewis dot diagram to work out the formula of hydrogen fluoride.

11. Draw a Lewis dot diagram to show that the formula of chlorine is Cl_2.

12. Draw a Lewis dot diagram to show that the formula of oxygen is O_2.

13. Draw a Lewis dot diagram to work out the formula of hydrogen sulfide.

14. Draw a Lewis dot diagram to show that the formula of nitrogen is N_2.

Answers to practice questions 7

1. H = [1]
2. C = [2,4]
3. N = [2,5]
4. O = [2,6]
5. F = [2,7]
6. Cl = [2,8,7]

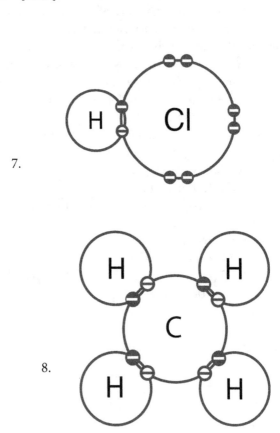

7.

8.

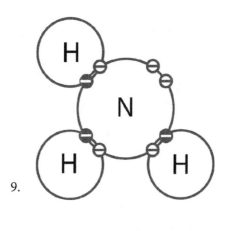

9.

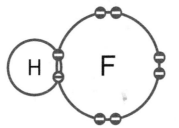

10.

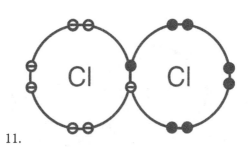

11.

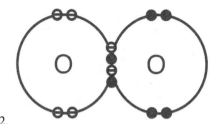

12.

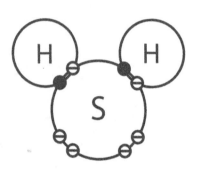

13.

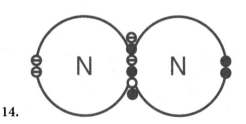

14.

Structures: giant and simple

Up until now the discussion was about how atoms join. Actually the particles (atoms or ions) may be arranged in two main different ways. Either, all the particles are joined together to make one huge structure, which is called a **giant structure** (or a macromolecular structure), or the particles join to make separate **simple** structures where a group of atoms join together to make one unit, called a molecule.

All **ionic** compounds always form a **giant** ionic structure of ions. Sometimes this is called an **ionic lattice**. Remember that ionic compounds are usually formed when metal atoms react with non-metals atoms. The ions stick together because opposite charges attract each other. The giant ionic lattice of sodium chloride ions is one example:

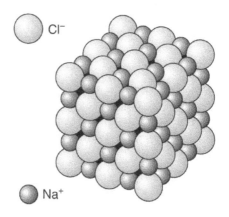

Cl^-

Na^+

All **metallic** elements and metallic mixtures (alloys) always form a **giant** structure of atoms, or more accurately a giant structure of cations (positive ions) in a sea of mobile electrons. Sometimes this is called a **metallic lattice**. The cations stay near each other because they are attracted to the shared mobile electrons. Here is an example of a giant metallic lattice:

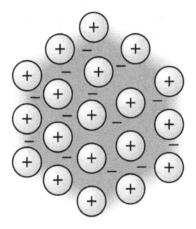

Covalent elements and compounds may form **giant** structures or **simple** covalent molecules. Remember that covalent compounds are only made of non-metal atoms. The atoms stick together because each atom's nucleus is attracted to the shared electrons in the covalent bonds.

Most **covalent elements**, and most covalent compounds, are made up of **simple covalent molecules**. Similarly to the example of hydrogen H_2, above, many non-metal elements form molecules made of two atoms. It is worth memorizing these elements with their formula: hydrogen H_2, oxygen O_2, nitrogen N_2, fluorine F_2, chlorine Cl_2, bromine Br_2, iodine I_2.

There are many examples of **covalent compounds** made of simple covalent molecules. Here are some common examples:

Methane, CH_4, is natural gas. This gas is piped to many homes, it is also a gas that forms in marshes. From the symbols it can be seen that methane molecules are made of one atom of carbon and four atoms of hydrogen.

Carbon dioxide, CO_2, is the gas we breathe out. The carbon dioxide molecules are made of one atom of carbon and two atoms of oxygen.

Ammonia, NH_3, which may be **given off when urine** decomposes, is a fertilizer, and is also **the gas given off** by old fashioned smelling salts. Ammonia molecules contain one atom of nitrogen and three atoms of hydrogen.

Sulfuric acid, H_2SO_4, is the acid in most car batteries. Sulfuric acid molecules contain two atoms of hydrogen, one of sulfur and four of oxygen.

Physical properties of elements and compounds

Bonding and structure, of elements and compounds, help to explain their melting points, boiling points, and electrical conductivity, all of which are sometimes called the physical properties.

Metallic physical properties

Metals may be found as pure metals, or as mixtures of metals, which are called **alloys**. Metals and alloys have the same general properties.

In general metals have a high melting point due to having a **giant** structure. The atoms or cations are held together by their strong attraction to the shared mobile electrons. In general most metals are solids at room temperature and strong. However mercury is a liquid at room temperature, and some metals, like sodium, are soft, because there are few mobile electrons holding the giant structure together and the atoms are large.

Metals conduct electricity when solid, and when liquid, because the electrons in the outer shells are **free to move** and so carry the charge.

Example: copper metal has a high melting point and is a good conductor of electricity, so copper is often used to make wires that conduct electricity.

Ionic physical properties

Ionic compounds always have a **high** melting point and boiling point because the ions are held together by **strong electrostatic forces**, and the ions are in a **giant** structure. It is important to emphasize that ionic compounds have the high melting and boiling points due to their **giant** structure.

Ionic liquids conduct electricity because in a liquid the **ions** are free to **move**, and so carry charge. **Ionic solids** do not conduct electricity because the ions are not free to move. Note that there are no free mobile electrons in an ionic liquid because the electrons are all held inside the ions. In a similar way **ionic solutions**, where an ionic compound (like common salt) is dissolved in water, also conduct electricity, because then the ions are free to move.
Ionic compounds are brittle because if the giant ionic lattice is hit then the ions shift, and so ions with the same charge align and so repel.

Example: sodium chloride, the common salt that we eat, has a high melting point and boiling point. When common salt is added to water, the water conducts electricity because the sodium ions and chloride ions are free to move.
Example: when sodium chloride is heated strongly then it does melt. This makes a molten ionic liquid, which conducts electricity because the sodium ions and chloride ions are mobile.

Covalent physical properties

The properties of covalent elements and compounds depend on whether they have a **giant** (macromolecular) or **simple** structure. Both types of covalent structures **do not conduct electricity** because the electrons are fixed in place.

Giant covalent structures have a **very high** melting point and boiling point because the atoms within the structures are joined together in one huge structure and those atoms are joined together by strong covalent bonds.

Example: diamond has a giant covalent structure so has a very high melting point and boiling point, and it does not conduct electricity. In addition the giant covalent structure explains why diamond is so hard.
Example: silicon dioxide, quartz, has a giant covalent structure like many rock forming minerals. Silicon dioxide is hard, has very high melting and boiling points, and does not conduct electricity.

Simple covalent structures have **low** melting points and boiling points because there are only **weak forces of attraction** between the covalently bonded molecules. Note that the atoms inside the molecules are held together by strong covalent bonds so when a simple covalent substance melts or boils the covalent bonds do not break. It is only the weak forces between the molecules that are overcome.

48

Example: when the compound water boils, the water molecules do not break, the covalent bonds do not break, instead the weak forces between the molecules are overcome, and are broken, so the molecules separate. The covalent bonds inside the molecules are not broken when water boils.

Example: the element nitrogen makes up most of the air around us. Nitrogen gas is made of molecules that contain two nitrogen atoms that are held together by strong covalent bonds. There are only weak forces attracting the molecules together. This explains why nitrogen is a gas at room temperature.

There is not room here to explain in full the nature of these weak forces between the molecules. The weak forces between molecules are actually weak electrostatic forces.

There are exceptions to the above patterns, though they are uncommon, but the exceptions are easily explained by studying the bonding and structure of the chemical substance.

Practice questions 8: Properties
1. Describe ionic compounds.
2. _____ compounds are held together by strong forces of attraction between oppositely charged ions . What is the missing word?
3. Why do the atoms in molecules stay together?

4. Which type of substance has a low melting point and does not conduct electricity?

5. Simple molecular compounds are gases, liquids or solids, which have relatively low melting points and boiling points. Why?

6. Which type of structure does diamond have?

7. Which type of structure does methane have?

8. State and explain the magnitude of diamond's melting point.

9. Which type of structure does silica (silicon dioxide) have?

10. Describe the bond arrangement in diamond.

11. Describe, in full, ionic structure.

12. State and explain the magnitude of sodium chloride's melting point.

13. State and explain when ionic compounds conduct electricity.

14. Which substances conduct electricity when they are melted or dissolved in water?

15. Describe and explain why metals conduct electricity.

16. What allows metal atoms to slide over each other in a solid? This allows metals to be easily shaped, malleable.

Answers to practice questions 8

1. They have a giant structure of ions held together by strong electrostatic attraction, due to the complete transfer of electrons. They have high melting and boiling points.

2. ionic

3. The atoms share pairs of electrons (covalent bonds). The nuclei in the atoms are attracted to the shared electrons.

4. simple molecular compounds

5. the intermolecular forces between the covalent molecules are weak

6. giant covalent structure (lattice) of atoms

7. simple covalent molecules

8. Due to the large number of covalent bonds in the giant 3D structure, diamond has a very high melting point.

9. giant covalent structure (lattice) of atoms

10. Each carbon atom forms four covalent bonds in a rigid, giant covalent structure.

11. Ions form a regular giant ionic structures in which there are strong electrostatic forces between oppositely charged ions.

12. Giant ionic structures have strong electrostatic forces between oppositely charged ions, so these compounds having high melting points.

13. When melted or dissolved in water, ionic compounds conduct electricity, because the ions are mobile.

14. giant ionic structures

15. because, in metals, the electrons are in the outer energy level (shell), and are mobile in all directions

16. because, in metals, the electrons in the outer energy level (shell) are mobile, so the atoms may slide past each other

How to write and balance a chemical equation

When chemical equations are written the reactants are written on the left and the products on the right. An arrow is used to indicate a reaction. Formulas are used to denote each of the chemical reactants and products. An explanation on how to write formulas will be found later on.

Matter cannot be created or destroyed, so the number of atoms of the reactants must equal the number of products. Large numbers are put just in front of each chemical formula to indicate multiples of the formula, and so balance the equation. Remember to write all the formulas of the reactants and products before trying to balance the equation. Usually, state symbols are added at the end.

Example: Hydrogen reacts with oxygen to make water. The formula of the element hydrogen is H_2; that of the element oxygen is O_2; and that of the compound water is H_2O.
The unbalanced equation would be:
$$H_2 + O_2 \rightarrow H_2O$$
As there are two oxygen atoms in one oxygen molecule, and only one oxygen atom in a water molecule, so the number of water molecules must be doubled:
$$H_2 + O_2 \rightarrow 2H_2O$$

Note that, usually, the equations include symbols indicating whether the chemicals are **solid (s), liquid (l),** or **gas (g)**. These are called the **state symbols**. Also, **(aq)** indicates that a substance is dissolved in water to form an '**aqueous**' solution. Note that (l) does not indicate that the chemical is dissolved in water.

As there are now four hydrogen atoms in the two water molecules so the number of reactant hydrogen molecules must be doubled to balance the equation:

$$2H_2 + O_2 \rightarrow 2H_2O$$

Usually state symbols are added and equation is complete:

$$2H_2(g) + O_2(g) \rightarrow 2H_2O(l)$$

If a substance is dissolved in water then it is said to be an aqueous solution, so (aq) is used as the state symbol.

Example: A solution of sodium chloride in water is written as NaCl(aq).

It is useful to remember that the chemicals at the start of a reaction are called the **reactants**. The chemicals produced are called the **products**.

What are reaction types?

Chemistry is the study of how one chemical changes into another chemical. When a chemical changes then that is called a reaction. When a reaction occurs bonds and ions are broken or formed, and new chemical substances are made.

One of the best ways to comprehend chemistry is to know the reaction types. This list of chemical reaction types, with explanations and examples, does not cover every reaction but does cover the most common of them.

Acids, bases, and salts

Acids contain hydrogen ions (H^+ ions) that can be replaced by metal ions. When the hydrogen ions of an acid are replaced by metal ions then a **salt** is formed. The acid is said to be **neutralized.**

Also, as described below, salts are also formed when ammonia neutralizes an acid.
Example: When sulfuric acid (which is in car batteries) reacts with iron then the salt, iron sulfate, is formed.

A compound that neutralizes an acid is called a **base**. For example, the base calcium oxide (quick lime) neutralizes sulfuric acid to make calcium sulfate.

The word **alkali** is used to describe a solution made when a base dissolves in water. **Alkalis** contain hydroxide ions (OH^-) .

Ions, acids and alkalis
When an acid (with H^+ ions) and an alkali (with OH^- ions) neutralize each other, then water is made:

$$H^+(aq) + OH^-(aq) \rightarrow H_2O(l)$$

This is called, **the ionic equation for neutralization**.

Here is a table of acids and the salts they make:

name	acid formula	salt made	sodium salt name	formula
sulfuric acid (battery acid)	H_2SO_4	sulfate	sodium sulfate	Na_2SO_4
nitric acid	HNO_3	nitrate	sodium nitrate	$NaNO_3$
hydrochloric acid (stomach acid)	HCl	chloride	sodium chloride	NaCl
ethanoic acid (vinegar)	CH_3COOH	ethanoate	sodium ethanoate	CH_3COONa

There are four main reactions of acids. Note that, also, ammonia neutralizes acids.

1) Metals and acid

When a **metal** reacts with an acid then a **salt** and **hydrogen** is formed. Note that some metals are not reactive enough to react with acid, for example copper (which is used to make water pipes), silver and gold:

$$\text{Metal} + \text{Acid} \rightarrow \text{Salt} + \text{Hydrogen}$$

Example: When magnesium reacts with sulfuric acid then the magnesium replaces the hydrogen in the acid to make the salt magnesium sulfate and hydrogen is given off:

magnesium + sulfuric acid $\rightarrow$ magnesium sulfate + hydrogen

$$Mg(s) + H_2SO_4(aq) \rightarrow MgSO_4(aq) + H_2(g)$$

Example: magnesium + hydrochloric acid $\rightarrow$ magnesium chloride + hydrogen

$$Mg(s) + 2HCl(aq) \rightarrow MgCl_2(aq) + H_2(g)$$

Example: magnesium + nitric acid $\rightarrow$ magnesium nitrate + hydrogen

$$Mg(s) + 2HNO_3(aq) \rightarrow Mg(NO_3)_2(aq) + H_2(g)$$

Remember:

$$\text{Metal} + \text{Acid} \rightarrow \text{Salt} + \text{Hydrogen}$$
which spells **MASH.**

2) Metal oxides and acid

When a **metal oxide** (a base) reacts with an **acid** then a **salt** and **water** is formed. Note that almost all metal oxides will react with acids, though the reaction may be slow.

$$\textbf{Metal Oxide + Acid} \rightarrow \textbf{Salt + Water}$$

Example: magnesium oxide + sulfuric acid →
magnesium sulfate + water

$$MgO(s) + H_2SO_4(aq) \rightarrow MgSO_4(aq) + H_2O(l)$$

Example: magnesium oxide + hydrochloric acid →
magnesium chloride + water

$$MgO(s) + 2HCl(aq) \rightarrow MgCl_2(aq) + H_2O(l)$$

Example: magnesium oxide + nitric acid →
magnesium nitrate + water

$$MgO(s) + 2HNO_3(aq) \rightarrow Mg(NO_3)_2(aq) + H_2O(l)$$

Remember:

$$\textbf{Metal Oxide + Acid} \rightarrow \textbf{Salt + Water.}$$

3) Metal hydroxides and acid

When a **metal hydroxide** (a base) reacts with an **acid** then a **salt** and **water** are formed. Note that almost all metal hydroxides will react with acids, though the reaction may be slow.

Metal Hydroxide + Acid → Salt + Water

Example:
magnesium hydroxide + sulfuric acid → magnesium sulfate + water

$$Mg(OH)_2(s) + H_2SO_4(aq) \rightarrow MgSO_4(aq) + 2H_2O(l)$$

Example:
sodium hydroxide + hydrochloric acid → sodium chloride + water

$$NaOH(aq) + HCl(aq) \rightarrow NaCl(aq) + H_2O(l)$$

Example:
sodium hydroxide + nitric acid → sodium nitrate + water

$$NaOH(aq) + HNO_3(aq) \rightarrow NaNO_3(aq) + H_2O(l)$$

Remember:

Metal Hydroxide + Acid → Salt + Water.

4) Metal carbonates and acid

When a **metal carbonate** (a base) reacts with an **acid** then **carbon dioxide** is formed as well as a **salt** and **water**. Note that almost all metal carbonates will react with acids and the mixture will **fizz** as the carbon dioxide comes off.

Metal Carbonate + Acid → Salt + Water + Carbon dioxide

Example: magnesium carbonate + sulfuric acid →
        magnesium sulfate + water + carbon dioxide

$$MgCO_3(s) + H_2SO_4(aq) \rightarrow MgSO_4(aq) + H_2O(l) + CO_2(g)$$

Example: sodium carbonate + hydrochloric acid →
        sodium chloride + water + carbon dioxide

$$Na_2CO_3(s) + 2HCl(aq) \rightarrow 2NaCl(aq) + H_2O(l) + CO_2(g)$$

Example: sodium carbonate + nitric acid → sodium
        nitrate + water + carbon dioxide

$$Na_2CO_3(s) + 2HNO_3(aq) \rightarrow 2NaNO_3(aq) + H_2O(l) + CO_2(g)$$

Remember:

Metal Carbonate + Acid → Salt + Water + Carbon dioxide

so **carbon**ates produce **carbon** dioxide

5) Ammonia and acid

Ammonia is a gas that is made of non-metal atoms, but it neutralizes acids. Molecules of **ammonia** contain one atom of **nitrogen** and three atoms of **hydrogen**, so the formula of ammonia is NH_3. When ammonia reacts with an acid it makes an ammonium salt. What occurs is that the ammonia removes the hydrogen from the acid to make an ammonium ion. The ammonium ion has one more hydrogen atom than ammonia and has a plus charge. Note that no water is produced.

Ammonia + Acid → Ammonium Salt

Example:

ammonia + sulfuric acid → ammonium sulfate

$$2NH_3(g) + H_2SO_4(aq) \rightarrow (NH_4)_2SO_4(aq)$$

Example:

ammonia + hydrochloric acid → ammonium chloride

$$NH_3(g) + HCl(aq) \rightarrow NH_4Cl(aq)$$

Example:

ammonia + nitric acid → ammonium nitrate

$$NH_3(g) + HNO_3(aq) \rightarrow NH_4NO_3(aq)$$

Remember:

Ammonia + Acid → Ammonium Salt

ammonia = NH_3
ammonium ion = NH_4^+

Practice questions 9: Acids, bases, and salts

1. What type of substances are bases?
2. What is a 'salt'?
3. Which ion is in all acids?
4. FINISH: Metal + acid → salt + ...
5. What is made when calcium oxide is reacted with nitric acid?
6. Alkalis, in aqueous solution, produce _____ ions.
7. Aqueous ammonia solution and sulfuric acid makes, what?
8. What is made when sodium hydroxide is reacted with hydrochloric acid?
9. What is the reaction type when sodium hydroxide reacts with hydrochloric acid?
10. Which is the ionic equation for neutralization?
11. When ammonia is dissolved, what type of solution is made?
12. What could fit in the gap?

   Acid + ... → Salt + Water.
13. Acids, in aqueous solution, produce _____.
14. How may salt copper (II) sulfate be made?
15. Aqueous ammonia solution and hydrochloric acid makes, what?
16. What type of substances contain H^+ ions?
17. How could iron (III) chloride be made?
18. Which ion is in alkalis?
19. Aqueous ammonia solution and nitric acid makes, what?
20. What is made when potassium hydroxide is reacted with sulfuric acid?
21. What type of substances contain OH^- ions?

Answers to practice questions 9

1. a metal oxide or hydroxide, or ammonia in solution
2. A salt is made when hydrogen ions of the acid are replaced by a metal or ammonium ions.
3. H^+ ions
4. hydrogen
5. calcium nitrate and water
6. OH^-
7. ammonium sulfate
8. water + sodium chloride
9. neutralization, also known as acid-base reaction
10. $H^+(aq) + OH^-(aq) \rightarrow H_2O(l)$
11. The gas ammonia dissolves to make an alkaline solution.
12. metal oxide or hydroxide
13. H^+ ions
14. Use a copper base to neutralize sulfuric acid. To dilute sulfuric acid add solid copper oxide, or copper carbonate, or copper hydroxide.
15. ammonium chloride
16. acids
17. Mix iron (III) hydroxide + dilute hydrochloric acid.
18. OH^- ions
19. ammonium nitrate
20. neutral potassium sulfate solution + water
21. alkalis

Oxidation and reduction

Oxidation and reduction are difficult to quickly comprehend because a full understanding depends on knowing the electronic structure of the ions and atoms that are involved. Also, the words themselves may be confusing until the historical background is outlined.

Sometimes **red**uction and **ox**idation reactions are called **redox reactions** for short.

Originally, **oxidation** meant that a substance had **gained oxygen**, so, for example, when charcoal (carbon) burns it gains oxygen to make carbon dioxide, so that burning (combustion) may be called oxidation.

Example: Copper metal may be heated in air to make copper oxide. This is oxidation:

$$copper + oxygen \rightarrow copper\ oxide$$
$$2Cu(s) + O_2(g) \rightarrow 2CuO(s)$$

Originally, **reduction** meant the **removal of oxygen**. Actually reduction was noticed before oxidation. When a metal is made, by heating a metal ore with charcoal, the mass of the metal formed was less than the ore. In other words the metal ore is reduced.

Example: The reduction of copper oxide using charcoal produces copper and carbon dioxide. The mass of the copper made is less than the mass of the original copper oxide:

copper oxide + carbon → copper + carbon dioxide
$$2CuO(s) + C(s) \rightarrow 2Cu(s) + CO_2(g)$$

Only later was it realized that reduction and oxidation were best described as the **gain or loss of electrons**. In the example of the reduction of copper oxide, the copper oxide is made of copper ions, Cu^{2+}, and oxide ions, O^{2-}. Each copper ion, Cu^{2+}, was changed into a copper atom, Cu. Remember: **electrons are negative**. So when reduced, each copper ion, Cu^{2+}, gains two electrons (to the carbon atoms) to become a neutral copper atom, Cu. So this is **reduction, the gain of electrons**.

Conversely, when copper is oxidized, by heating in air, then the copper atoms, Cu, loses two electrons (to the oxygen atoms) to become copper ions, Cu^{2+}. So, this is **oxidation, the loss of electrons**.

Remember:

Oxidation **I**s the **L**oss of electrons (**OIL**)

Reduction **I**s the **G**ain of electrons (**RIG**)

This is the most difficult reaction type for students of chemistry to recognize. Perhaps it is useful to remember that when a **metal** reacts to form a compound then the metal atoms **lose electrons**, so are **oxidized** and form **positive** ions. The opposite is also true. When metal ions are converted back into atoms then the metal ions gain electrons, and are reduced.

Also, generally, when a **non-metal** reacts, the non-metal atoms **gain electrons**, and are **reduced** to make **negative** ions. The opposite is also true. When non-metal ions, which are negative, are converted back into atoms, then the negative ions lose negative electrons, so are oxidized.

Hydrogen is a special non-metal. Usually, when hydrogen reacts the hydrogen atoms lose electrons to become hydrogen ions which have a positive charge, H^+. Of course, hydrogen ions may gain electrons, be reduced, and so become hydrogen again.

xidation and reduction

ı terms of electrons?

ı, in terms of electrons?

ıetal atoms react they form zinc 2+

ıype of reaction is this?

ı zinc 2+ ions react they form zinc atoms.

ıt type of reaction is this?

ɔ. When chlorine atoms form ions they form chloride ions (Cl^-). What type of reaction is this?

6. When chloride ions react they may form chlorine atoms. What type of reaction is this?

7. What type of reaction is it when hydrogen ions (H+ ions) react to form hydrogen gas.

8. Aluminium is made by passing electricity through a liquid that contains aluminium 3+ ions. Aluminium atoms are made. What type of reaction is this?

9. For iron(II)oxide to be made from iron, oxygen must be added. Is the iron oxidized or reduced?

10. When copper(II)sulfate solution reacts with zinc metal then zinc sulfate solution and brown copper is made. What has happened to the zinc metal and the copper(II) ions?

Answers to practice questions 10

1. Oxidation is the loss of electrons.
2. Reduction is the gain of electrons.
3. oxidation
4. reduction
5. reduction
6. oxidation
7. Reduction. The hydrogen 1+ ions gain electro
form hydrogen atoms which join in pairs to form
hydrogen molecules.
8. reduction
9. oxidized
10. The zinc atoms have been oxidized to zinc 2+ ions,
and the copper 2+ ions have been reduced to copper
atoms.

Other reaction types

Thermal decomposition

Heating some compounds **break** them down into other chemicals. Look for only one reactant and more than one product. Also note that **thermal** decomposition requires **heat**.

Example: heating limestone, solid calcium carbonate, produces solid calcium oxide and carbon dioxide gas:

$$\text{calcium carbonate} \rightarrow \text{calcium oxide} + \text{carbon dioxide}$$
$$CaCO_3(s) \rightarrow CaO(s) + CO_2(g)$$

Example: Crude oil is made of hydrocarbons (covalent molecules made of only carbon and hydrogen). The long chain molecules may be broken to make more useful short chain molecules using thermal decomposition. This is usually called **cracking**.

For example decane could be broken down to make octane (petrol) and ethene (which could be used to make polyethene):

$$\text{decane} \rightarrow \text{octane} + \text{ethene}$$
$$C_{10}H_{22} \rightarrow C_8H_{18} + C_2H_4$$

Exothermic - burning, respiration

Some reactions give off energy, usually heat. Generally, this causes the temperature to increase. It gets hot. This type of reaction is said to be **exothermic**.

Example: Burning a fuel in air (actually oxygen) produces heat. Another word for burning is **combustion**. Burning is exothermic.

> Note that **boiling** does not mean burning - it means changing a liquid into a gas.

The fuel methane (natural gas) reacts with the oxygen in the air to produce carbon dioxide and water:

Methane + oxygen → carbon dioxide + water vapour
(and heat)
$$CH_4(g) + 2O_2(g) \rightarrow CO_2(g) + 2H_2O(g)$$

Example: Much of the food we eat slowly reacts with oxygen to produce energy including heat. This is called **respiration**. The simple sugar glucose reacts with oxygen to make carbon dioxide, water and energy:

glucose + oxygen → carbon dioxide + water (& energy)
$$C_6H_{12}O_6(s) + 6O_2(g) \rightarrow 6CO_2(g) + 6H_2O(l)$$

Example: Some water contains health giving calcium ions, perhaps the water contains soluble calcium sulfate. If washing soda (sodium carbonate) is added to the hard water then the water goes cloudy because insoluble calcium carbonate forms:

soluble sodium carbonate + soluble calcium sulfate → **insoluble** calcium carbonate solid + soluble sodium sulfate

$$Na_2CO_3(aq) + CaSO_4(aq) \rightarrow \textbf{CaCO}_3\textbf{(s)} + Na_2SO_4(aq)$$

The **insoluble** solid formed is called a **precipitate**.

Practice questions 11: Reaction types

1. Limescale (calcium carbonate) may be removed by reacting it with vinegar (ethanoic acid). What type of reaction is this?

2. Soda crystals (sodium carbonate) in water react with **grease** (fatty acids) so that they may be washed away. What type of reaction is this?

3. In a house fire, when wood and plastic are heated in limited air, poisonous carbon monoxide and hydrogen cyanide are often formed. What type of reaction is this?

4. Bleach usually contains an oxygen rich compound that removes electrons from microbes which kills them. What type of reaction is this?

5. The best silver cleaners change the silver tarnish, which contains silver 1+ ions, back into silver. What type of reaction is this?

6. When common salt (sodium chloride) is added to

ice the temperature rapidly falls as the ice melts. What type of change is this?

7 To soften tap water for washing, you could add washing soda (sodium carbonate) . A harmless cloud of solid calcium carbonate would appear. What type of reaction is this?

8. In plants, many sugar molecules are joined together to make huge starch molecules. What type of reaction is this?

9. In a mobile phone battery a chemical reaction produces electricity. When the battery is recharged the chemical reaction is forced to go backwards. What type of reaction is this?

10. When black solid copper (II) oxide is warmed with sulfuric acid then a blue copper (II) sulfate solution is made. What type of reaction is this?

Answers to practice questions 11

1. acid-base (neutralization)
2. acid-base (neutralization)
3. thermal decomposition
4. oxidation of the microbes; reduction of the bleach; a redox reaction
5. reduction of the silver 1+ ions; oxidation of the cleaner; a redox reaction
6. endothermic change
7 precipitation
8. polymerization
9. reversible (and it is also a redox reaction)
10. acid-base (neutralization)

Chemical formulas

Ionic formula

Ionic formulas do not have to be memorized. If the formula and the charges of each ion are learnt, then the ionic formula may be worked out as required.
A table of ions follows this explanation of how to work out formulas.

These worked examples show you how to work out ionic formulas:

Example: What is the formula of magnesium chloride?
The ions in magnesium chloride are Mg^{2+} and Cl^-.
The magnesium ion has a 2+ charge.
The chloride ion has a 1 - charge.
The number of positive charges must equal the number of negative charges,
so there must be two chloride ions for each magnesium ion.
This is written as $MgCl_2$. The 2 is written to the right and below the Cl to indicate that there are two Cls.
There is only one Mg.
So the formula of magnesium chloride is $MgCl_2$.

Example: What is the formula of lithium oxide?
The ions in lithium oxide are Li^+ and O^{2-}.
The number of plus charges must equal the number of negative charges,

so there must be two lithium ions for each oxide ion.
So the formula of lithium oxide is Li_2O.

Example: What is the formula of aluminium oxide?
The ions in aluminium oxide are Al^{3+} and O^{2-}.
There must be two aluminium ions for every three oxide ions.
So the formula of aluminium oxide is Al_2O_3.

Example: What is the formula of calcium carbonate?
The ions in calcium carbonate are Ca^{2+} and CO_3^{2-}.
There must be one calcium ion for each carbonate ion.
So the formula of calcium carbonate is $CaCO_3$.

Example: What is the formula of ammonium nitrate?
The ions in ammonium nitrate are NH_4^+ and NO_3^-.
There must be one ammonium ion for each nitrate ion.
So the formula of ammonium nitrate is NH_4NO_3.

Example: What is the formula of calcium hydroxide?
The ions in calcium oxide are Ca^{2+} and OH^-.
There must be one calcium ion for each two hydroxide ions.
So the formula of calcium carbonate is $Ca(OH)_2$.
This time brackets must be used to show that two hydroxide ions are present.
Without brackets this formula $CaOH_2$would be wrong as it suggest that there is only one oxygen atom in the formula.

...ormula of ammonium sulfate?
...lfate are NH_4^+ and SO_4^{2-}.
...ium ions for each sulfate

...mmonium sulfate is $(NH_4)_2SO_4$.

Formula of ions

...e most common ions are listed below. Note
...ny metal ions have the same charge as their
...p number.

1+ ions	2+ ions	3+ ions	2- ions	1- ions
Li^+			O^{2-}	F^-
Na^+	Mg^{2+}	Al^{3+}	S^{2-}	Cl^-
K^+	Ca^{2+}			Br^-
	Ba^{2+}			I^-
H^+	Fe^{2+}	Fe^{3+}	CO_3^{2-}	OH^-
NH_4^+	Cu^{2+}		SO_4^{2-}	NO_3^-

Note that the negative ions that include an element
with oxygen have different endings to their name. The
S^{2-} ion is the **sulfide** ion, whereas the SO_4^{2-} ion is the
sulfate ion.

Also note that the gas **ammonia** is NH_3, while the
ammonium ion is NH_4^+.

Practice questions 12: Ionic formula

1. What is the formula of sodium chloride?
2. What is the formula of calcium chloride?
3. What is the formula of aluminium chloride?
4. What is the formula of sodium oxide?
5. What is the formula of calcium oxide?
6. What is the formula of aluminium oxide?
7. What is the formula of sodium hydroxide?
8. What is the formula of calcium hydroxide?
9. What is the formula of iron (III) hydroxide?
10. What is the formula of sodium carbonate?
11. What is the formula of calcium carbonate?
12. What is the formula of aluminium carbonate?
13. What is the formula of sodium sulfate?
14. What is the formula of calcium sulfate?
15. What is the formula of potassium sulfate?
16. What is the formula of potassium nitrate?
17. What is the formula of magnesium sulfate?

Answers to practice questions 12

1. $NaCl$
2. $CaCl_2$
3. $AlCl_3$
4. Na_2O
5. CaO
6. Al_2O_3
7. $NaOH$
8. $Ca(OH)_2$
9. $Fe(OH)_3$

10. Na_2CO_3

11. $CaCO_3$

12. $Al_2(CO_3)_3$

13. Na_2SO_4

14. $CaSO_4$

15. K_2SO_4

16. KNO_3

17. $MgSO_4$

Covalent formulas

To work out the formula of a covalent compound a Lewis dot diagram (dot and cross diagram) is used. This will show how many atoms of each of the elements will join together to make a molecule. As a general rule most non-metal atoms will make a fixed number of bonds.

H atoms make 1 bond.

C atoms 4 bonds

N atoms 3 bonds

O atoms 2 bonds

F atoms 1 bond

Cl atoms 1 bond

Water, H_2O, is an example of a covalent molecule. Each oxygen atom will make two bonds, and each hydrogen atom makes one covalent bond, so one oxygen atom joins to two hydrogen atoms. This is best shown in a Lewis dot diagram:

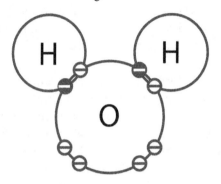

A water molecule could also be shown as sticks for bonds and symbols as atoms:

In this way, the structure, and so the formula, of different covalent molecules may be drawn.

Practice questions 13: Covalent formulas

1. What is the formula of hydrogen sulfide (the smell of bad eggs)?

2. Sulfur dioxide may trigger asthma. What is its formula? (Hint: Here, sulfur makes four bonds)

3. Natural gas is methane, a carbon hydride. What is its formula? (Hint: one C atom in each molecule)

4. What is the formula of carbon dioxide (a gas which we breathe out)?

5. What is the formula of hydrogen chloride (a gas which dissolves in water to make hydrochloric acid)?

6. Ammonia (nitrogen hydride) is found in smelling salts, oven cleaners, and some hair products. What is its formula? (Hint: one N atom in each molecule)

7. What is the formula of the explosive compound, nitrogen chloride? (Hint: one N atom in each molecule)

8. Carbon disulfide smells of rotting cabbage. What is its formula?

9. What is the formula of carbon tetrachloride, once used in dry cleaning until it was realized that it was destroying the ozone layer?

10. What is the formula of hydrogen carbon nitride, which is known as, the very poisonous, hydrogen cyanide?

Answers to practice questions 13

1. H_2S 2. SO_2 3. CH_4 4. CO_2 5. HCl

6. NH_3 7. NCl_3 8. CS_2 9. CCl_4 10. HCN

Endothermic - photosynthesis, evaporation

Some reactions take in energy, often as heat. This usually causes the temperature to decrease. It gets cold. This reaction type is said to be endothermic.

Example: The thermal decomposition reactions discussed earlier are endothermic reactions:

calcium carbonate → calcium oxide + carbon dioxide
$$CaCO_3(s) \quad \rightarrow \quad CaO(s) \quad + \quad CO_2(g)$$

decane → octane + ethene
$$C_{10}H_{22} \rightarrow C_8H_{18} + C_2H_4$$

Example: Another example is **photosynthesis,** which is when plants (or algae) take in light energy, carbon dioxide and water to make sugar and oxygen. In this example glucose is made:

carbon dioxide + water (& light) → glucose + oxygen
$$6CO_2(g) \quad + \quad 6H_2O(l) \quad \rightarrow \quad C_6H_{12}O_6(s) + 6O_2(g)$$

Example: Evaporation is an endothermic physical (not chemical) change. Liquid water turns into gaseous water, called water vapour:

liquid water → gaseous water vapour
$$H_2O(l) \rightarrow H_2O(g)$$

Reversible reactions

Some reactions are reversible. They are indicated by using a double headed arrow such as '$\rightleftharpoons$'. This means the reaction will go both from the reactants to products, and from the products to the reactants.

Example: Respiration is effectively the reverse of photosynthesis. (see earlier).

Example: Thermal decomposition of calcium carbonate may be reversed. When carbon dioxide gas flows over calcium oxide then solid calcium carbonate is formed:

calcium oxide + carbon dioxide $\rightarrow$ calcium carbonate
$$CaO(s) + CO_2(g) \rightarrow CaCO_3(s)$$

So, if calcium carbonate was heated in a sealed metal box then the compound would both decompose and reform:

calcium oxide + carbon dioxide $\rightleftharpoons$ calcium carbonate
$$CaO(s) + CO_2(g) \rightleftharpoons CaCO_3(s)$$

Polymerization

When many small molecules (monomers) join together to form long molecules (polymers) then that is polymerization. Polymers are commonly called 'plastics.' **Example:** ethene molecules join to make polyethene, more commonly known as polythene. Polyethene molecules many be thousands, or hundreds of thousands, of atoms long:

ethene $\rightarrow$ polyethene (also called polyethylene)

many $C_2H_4 \rightarrow$ -[-CH_2CH_2-]- (which represents a small part of the very long molecule). This represents is a longer piece:

-[-$CH_2CH_2CH_2CH_2CH_2CH_2CH_2CH_2CH_2CH_2$-]-

Solutions, solubility, solvent and solute

When common salt (sodium chloride) is dissolved in water then a salt **solution** forms. Water dissolves salt, so water is called a **solvent**. The salt is dissolved, so salt is called the **solute**. So, a **solvent** dissolves a **solute** to make a **solution**. If a substance does not dissolve in the solvent then it is said to be **insoluble**.

Salt dissolving could be shown as a reaction:

$$\text{salt} + \text{water} \rightarrow \text{salt solution}$$
$$NaCl(s) + H_2O\ (l) \rightarrow NaCl(aq)$$

or

$$NaCl(s) + (aq) \rightarrow NaCl(aq)$$

Example: Sugar dissolves in water to make a sugar solution. The sugar is the solute. Water is the solvent. Sugar is soluble in water.

Example: Perfume dissolves in alcohol. The alcohol is the solvent, the perfume is the solute. When worn the alcohol evaporates leaving the perfume which evaporates very slowly.

Example: Candle wax is insoluble in water. Candle wax, the solute, will dissolve in petrol, the solvent.

Example: Nail varnish is insoluble in water, but it does dissolve in some solvents, for example propanone (acetone) or ethylethanoate (ethyl ester).

Solubility rules

Many ionic compounds dissolve in water because the water molecules are polar. This means that the hydrogen atoms are slightly positive and the oxygen atoms are slightly negative because the oxygen atoms are attractive to electrons. These partial charges attract the ions. The positive ions are attracted to the negative oxygen atoms, while the negative ions are attracted to the positive hydrogen atoms.

As a rule, all group 1, and ammonium compounds, are soluble.
All nitrates are soluble.
Most chlorides are soluble, though silver chloride and lead (II) chloride are insoluble.
Most sulfates are soluble, though barium and strontium sulfates are insoluble, as is lead (II) sulfate.
Most oxides, and hydroxides are insoluble, though group 1 and ammonium hydroxides are insoluble.

As a general rule covalent molecules do not dissolve in water. Most organic molecules are not polar and so are not attractive to water. However some are polar and do dissolve, but they are beyond the scope of this book.

Precipitation and salts

If two solutions are mixed then often all that will form is a mixture. Sometimes one ion, from one solution, will join with an ion from the other solution to form an insoluble solid, called a **precipitate**.

A full periodic table

Period / **Group**

Group 1	Group 2

Key

Relative Atomic Mass
Symbol
Name
Atomic number

Period 1

1
H
Hydrogen
1

Period 2

7	9
Li	**Be**
Lithium	Beryllium
3	4

Period 3

23	24
Na	**Mg**
Sodium	Magnesium
11	12

Period 4

39	40	45	48	51	52	55	56	59
K	**Ca**	**Sc**	**Ti**	**V**	**Cr**	**Mn**	**Fe**	**Co**
Potassium	Calcium	Scandium	Titanium	Vanadium	Chromium	Manganese	Iron	Cobalt
19	20	21	22	23	24	25	26	27

Period 5

85	88	89	91	93	96	99	101	103
Rb	**Sr**	**Y**	**Zr**	**Nb**	**Mo**	**Tc**	**Ru**	**Rh**
Rubidium	Strontium	Yttrium	Zirconium	Niobium	Molybdenum	Technetium	Ruthenium	Rhodium
37	38	39	40	41	42	43	44	45

Period 6

133	137	139	178	181	184	186	190	192
Cs	**Ba**	**La**	**Hf**	**Ta**	**W**	**Re**	**Os**	**Ir**
Caesium	Barium	Lanthanum	Hafnium	Tantalum	Tungsten	Rhenium	Osmium	Iridium
55	56	57	72	73	74	75	76	77

Period 7

223	226	227
Fr	**Ra**	**Ac**
Francium	Radium	Actinium
87	88	89

140	141	144	(147)	150	152
Ce	**Pr**	**Nd**	**Pm**	**Sm**	**Eu**
Cerium	Praseodymium	Neodymium	Promethium	Samarium	Europium
58	59	60	61	62	63
232	(231)	238	(237)	(242)	(243)
Th	**Pa**	**U**	**Np**	**Pu**	**Am**
Thorium	Protactinium	Uranium	Neptunium	Plutonium	Americium
90	91	92	93	94	95

Periodic Table

	Group					
	3	**4**	**5**	**6**	**7**	**8**	Period

Group 3	Group 4	Group 5	Group 6	Group 7	Group 8	Period
					4 **He** Helium 2	1
11 **B** Boron 5	12 **C** Carbon 6	14 **N** Nitrogen 7	16 **O** Oxygen 8	19 **F** Fluorine 9	20 **Ne** Neon 10	2
27 **Al** Aluminium 13	28 **Si** Silicon 14	31 **P** Phosphorus 15	32 **S** Sulphur 16	35.5 **Cl** Chlorine 17	40 **Ar** Argon 18	3

			Group 3	Group 4	Group 5	Group 6	Group 7	Group 8	Period
59 **Ni** Nickel 28	63.5 **Cu** Copper 29	65.4 **Zn** Zinc 30	70 **Ga** Gallium 31	73 **Ge** Germanium 32	75 **As** Arsenic 33	79 **Se** Selenium 34	80 **Br** Bromine 35	84 **Kr** Krypton 36	4
106 **Pd** Palladium 46	108 **Ag** Silver 47	112 **Cd** Cadmium 48	115 **In** Indium 49	119 **Sn** Tin 50	122 **Sb** Antimony 51	128 **Te** Tellurium 52	127 **I** Iodine 53	131 **Xe** Xenon 54	5
195 **Pt** Platinum 78	197 **Au** Gold 79	201 **Hg** Mercury 80	204 **Tl** Thallium 81	207 **Pb** Lead 82	209 **Bi** Bismuth 83	210 **Po** Polonium 84	210 **At** Astatine 85	222 **Rn** Radon 86	6

7

157 **Gd** Gadolinium 64	159 **Tb** Terbium 65	163 **Dy** Dysprosium 66	165 **Ho** Holmium 67	167 **Er** Erbium 68	169 **Tm** Thulium 69	173 **Yb** Ytterbium 70	175 **Lu** Lutetium 71
(247) **Cm** Curium 96	(245) **Bk** Berkelium 97	(251) **Cf** Californium 98	(254) **Es** Einsteinium 99	(253) **Fm** Fermium 100	(256) **Md** Mendelevium 101	(254) **No** Nobelium 102	(257) **Lr** Lawrencium 103